Table of Contents

Easy Preserving Recipes

    Recipe 1: Classic Fiesta Salsa

    Recipe 2: Tasty Onion and Pepper Relish

    Recipe 3: Sweet Persimmon Jam

    Recipe 4: Easy Preserved Sauerkraut

    Recipe 5: Sweet Crabapple Jelly

    Recipe 6: Watermelon Style Pickles

    Recipe 7: Pear Flavored Butter

    Recipe 8: Roasted Red Pepper Jam

    Recipe 9: Chipotle Style Plum Sauce

    Recipe 10: Rummage Style Relish

    Recipe 11: Spicy Style Tomato Jam

    Recipe 12: Simple Cranberry Butter

    Recipe 13: Classic Banana Jam

    Recipe 14: Acorn Squash Style Butter

    Recipe 15: Preserved Carrots and Jalapenos

    Recipe 16: Healthy Chia Seed Jam

    Recipe 17: Budget Friendly Berry Jam

    Recipe 18: Ginger Flavored Marmalade

    Recipe 19: Fresh Tasting Papaya Jam

    Recipe 20: Simple Gooseberry Jam

Recipe 21: Harvest Time Tomato Marinara Sauce

Recipe 22: Carolina Style BBQ Peppers

Recipe 23: Sweet Tasting Kiwi Jam

Recipe 24: Fresh Watermelon Preserves

Recipe 25: Garlic Flavored Pickles

Easy Preserving Recipes

Recipe 1: Classic Fiesta Salsa

If you are a huge fan of salsa, then I know you are certainly going to love this recipe. For the tastiest results I highly recommend serving this delicious salsa with some tortilla chips at your next gathering. I am sure your guests will love it too.

Yield: 32 Servings

Cooking Time: 1 ½ Hours

List of Ingredients:

- 4 ½ Cups of Tomatoes, Fresh and Finely Diced
- 3 Tablespoons of Vinegar, White
- ¼ Cup of Salsa, Your Favorite Kind
- 2, 16 Ounces of Canning Jars, With Lids and Rings

AAAAAAAAAAAAAAAAAAAAAAAAAAAAAAAAAAAAAAAAAAAAAAAAAAAAA

Instructions:

1. The first thing that you will want to do is combine your diced tomatoes, vinegar and favorite kind of salsa in a large sized saucepan placed over medium heat.

2. Cook your mixture until boiling. Once your mixture is boiling reduce the heat to low and allow to simmer for the next 5 minutes.

3. Remove from heat and allow to cool completely.

4. Pour your mixture into your canning jars and seal with your lids.

5. Boil your jars in some boiling water for the next 10 minutes. Remove and allow to cool slightly before placing into your fridge. Use whenever you are ready.

Recipe 2:   Tasty Onion and Pepper Relish

This is the perfect recipe to make if you want to put relish on nearly every dish that you make. It is very easy to make and contains a touch of spice that I know you won't be able to resist.

Yield: 128 Servings

Cooking Time: 5 Hours and 10 Minutes

List of Ingredients:

- 3 Onions, Large in Size and Sliced Thinly
- 8 Bell Peppers, Green in Color and Sliced into Thin Strips
- 3 Jalapeno Peppers, Seeded and Minced
- 6 Tablespoons of Spice, Pickled Variety
- 2 Cups of Sugar, White
- 1 teaspoon of Salt, For Taste
- 2 Cups of Vinegar, Apple Cider Variety

AAAAAAAAAAAAAAAAAAAAAAAAAAAAAAAAAAAAAAAAAAAAAAAAAAAAA

Instructions:

1. The first thing that you want to do is place all of your ingredients into a large sized saucepan.

2. Bring this mixture to a boil over high heat. Once your mixture is boiling reduce the heat to low and allow to simmer for the next 5 minutes, making sure that you stir occasionally.

3. Remove from heat and allow to cool completely.

4. Pour your mixture into your canning jars and seal with your lids.

5. Boil your jars in some boiling water for the next 10 minutes. Remove and allow to cool slightly before placing into your fridge. Use whenever you are ready.

Recipe 3:   Sweet Persimmon Jam

This is a great tasting jam that you won't be able to resist once you get a taste of it yourself. This jam is made with a perfect combination of lemon juice, zest from an orange, nutmeg, persimmons and sugar, making it the perfect treat to help satisfy your sweet tooth.

Yield: 48 Servings

Cooking Time: 40 Minutes

List of Ingredients:

- 5 Cups of Persimmons, Pureed Variety
- 3 Cups of Sugar, White
- ¼ Cup of Lemon Juice, Fresh
- ½ teaspoons of Orange Zest, Freshly Grated
- Dash of Nutmeg, Ground Variety

AAAAAAAAAAAAAAAAAAAAAAAAAAAAAAAAAAAAAAAAAAAAAAAAAAAA

Instructions:

1. Use a large sized saucepan and place over medium to high heat.

2. Add in all of your ingredients into your saucepan and bring to a boil.

3. Boil for the next 30 minutes or until your mixture is thick in consistency.

4. Remove from heat and allow to cool completely.

5. Pour your mixture into your canning jars and seal with your lids.

6. Boil your jars in some boiling water for the next 10 minutes. Remove and allow to cool slightly before placing into your fridge. Use whenever you are ready.

Recipe 4: Easy Preserved Sauerkraut

If you are a huge fan of sauerkraut, then I know you are going to fall in love with this recipe. Once you get a taste of this sauerkraut for yourself, I know you are going to want to serve it on everything.

Yield: 144 Servings

Cooking Time: 2 Hours and 30 Minutes

List of Ingredients:

- 50 Pounds of Cabbage, Fresh
- 1 Pound of Salt, Canning Variety

AAAAAAAAAAAAAAAAAAAAAAAAAAAAAAAAAAAAAAAAAAAAAAAAAAA

Instructions:

1. First remove the outer leaves from your cabbage. Then wash it thoroughly and set aside to drain. Once drain chop up your cabbage into quarters, making sure to remove the core.

2. Then use a large sized bowl and mix your salt with your cabbage.

3. Allow you cabbage to sit for the next couple of minutes or until completely wilted.

4 Pack your cabbage into your canning jars and repeat until all of your cabbage has been canned.

5. Boil your jars in some boiling water for the next 10 minutes. Remove and allow to cool slightly before placing into your fridge. Use whenever you are ready.

Recipe 5:   Sweet Crabapple Jelly

This is a great tasting and sweet jelly recipe that I know you are going to love. The best part about this preserving recipe is that you do not need to add in pectin to make this dish.

Yield: 32 Servings

Cooking Time: 15 Minutes

List of Ingredients:

- 8 Cups of Crabapples, Fresh
- Some Water, As Needed
- 3 Cups of Sugar, White
- 1, 3 Inch Stick of Cinnamon, Optional

AAAAAAAAAAAAAAAAAAAAAAAAAAAAAAAAAAAAAAAAAAAAAAAAAAA

Instructions:

1. The first thing that you will want to do is remove the stems and blossoms from your crabapples and then cut them into quarters. Place into a large sized saucepan.

2. Add in some water to cover and bring to a boil over medium heat. Allow to boil for the next 10 to 15 minutes or until they are tender to the touch.

3. After this time strain your apples and juice them. Discard any pulp and place your juice back into your pan.

4. Heat over low heat and allow to cook for the next 10 minutes. After this time skim off any foam that may appear on the top of your mixture.

5. Add in your sugar and stir thoroughly until completely dissolved.

6. Boil for the next 20 minutes before removing from heat. Allow to cool completely.

7. Pour your mixture into your canning jars and seal with your lids.

8. Boil your jars in some boiling water for the next 10 minutes. Remove and allow to cool slightly before placing into your fridge. Use whenever you are ready.

Recipe 6:   Watermelon Style Pickles

This is a great tasting pickle recipe that you can make during the hot summer months. Feel free to serve this dish as a tasty treat or to be used as a condiment for your next sandwich or hoagie that you may make.

Yield: 24 Servings

Cooking Time: 21 Hours and 15 Minutes

List of Ingredients:

- 1 Cup of Salt, Canning Variety
- 1 Gallon of Water, Cold
- 16 Cups of Watermelon Rind, Cut into Cubes
- 1 Gallon of Water, Cold
- 3 Sticks of Cinnamon
- 1 teaspoon of Allspice, Whole
- 1 teaspoon of Cloves, Whole
- 2 Cups of Vinegar, White
- 3 Cups of Sugar, White
- 12 Cherries, Maraschino Variety and Cut into Halves
- 6, 1 Pint Canning Jars, With Lids and Rings

AAAAAAAAAAAAAAAAAAAAAAAAAAAAAAAAAAAAAAAAAAAAAAAAAAAAAAA

Instructions:

1. The first thing that you will want to do is stir your salt into your gallon of water in a large sized container until it is completely dissolved. Add in your watermelon rind then cover with some plastic wrap and allow to sit for the next 12 hours. After this time drain and rinse completely.

2. Next place your remaining gallon of water and watermelon rind into a large sized stock pot. Set over medium heat and bring to a boil. Once boiling reduce the heat to low and continue to simmer for the next 45 minutes to an hour or until your rind is tender to the touch.

3. Add in your next 3 ingredients into a spice bag and submerge into your pot.

4. Add in your remaining ingredients and stir to combine. Reduce the heat to low and allow to simmer for the next 5 to 10 minutes.

5. After this time remove your spice bag and remove your mixture from heat. Allow to cool completely.

6. Pour your mixture into your canning jars and seal with your lids.

7. Boil your jars in some boiling water for the next 10 minutes. Remove and allow to cool slightly before placing into your fridge. Use whenever you are ready.

Recipe 7: Pear Flavored Butter

This delicious butter recipe is lightly scented with some fresh orange and nutmeg, making it a butter recipe that I know you won't soon forget. I know you are going to want to serve it constantly on some toast or even with your next dinner meal.

Yield: 32 Servings

Cooking Time: 31 Minutes

List of Ingredients:

- 4 Pounds of Pears, Medium in Size, Cored and Cut into Quarters
- 2 Cups of Sugar, White
- 1 teaspoon of Orange Zest, Finely Grated
- ¼ teaspoons of Nutmeg, Ground
- ¼ Cup of Orange Juice, Fresh

AAAAAAAAAAAAAAAAAAAAAAAAAAAAAAAAAAAAAAAAAAAAAAAAAAAAAAAA

Instructions:

1. The first thing that you will want to do is place your pears into a large sized pot placed over medium heat. Add in water to cover your bears and cook until they are tender to the touch. This should take 30 minutes.

2. After this time remove your pears and press through a sieve, Hold onto your pulp.

3. Place your pear pulp into a large sized saucepan along with your sugar and stir thoroughly until your sugar fully dissolves.

4. Add in your remaining ingredients and cook this mixture over medium heat until it is thick in consistency. Cook for the next hour.

5. Pour your mixture into your canning jars and seal with your lids. Allow to cool completely.

6. Pour your mixture into your canning jars and seal with your lids.

7. Boil your jars in some boiling water for the next 10 minutes. Remove and allow to cool slightly before placing into your fridge. Use whenever you are ready.

Recipe 8: Roasted Red Pepper Jam

While I know that roasted red pepper jam may seem far from appetizing, you will not think the same once you get a taste of this delicious spread for yourself. It not only tastes amazing, but it looks just as appetizing as well.

Yield: 30 Servings

Cooking Time: 1 ½ Hours

List of Ingredients:

- 6 Pounds of Bell Peppers, Red in Color
- 1 Pound of Tomatoes, Plum and Italian Variety
- 2 Cloves of Garlic, Unpeeled
- 1 White Onion, Small in Size and Sliced Thinly
- ½ Cup of Vinegar, Red Wine Variety
- 2 Tablespoons of Basil, Fresh and Finely Chopped
- 1 tablespoon of Sugar, White
- 1 teaspoon of Salt, For Taste
- 5 Canning Jars, With Lids and Rings

AAAAAAAAAAAAAAAAAAAAAAAAAAAAAAAAAAAAAAAAAAAAAAAAAAAA

Instructions:

1. The first thing that you will want to do is roast your first 4 ingredients in your oven at 425 degrees until your ingredients are soft and black in color on all sides. Once black, remove from oven.

2. Allow your ingredients to cool completely before placing into a food processor and blending on the highest setting until smooth in consistency.

3. Place your mixture into a large sized saucepan and add in your remaining ingredients. Stir until completely combined. Heat over medium heat and bring this mixture to a boil.

4. Once your mixture is boiling, reduce the heat to low and allow to simmer for the next 20 minutes. Remove from heat and allow to cool completely.

5. Pour your mixture into your canning jars and seal with your lids.

6. Boil your jars in some boiling water for the next 10 minutes. Remove and

allow to cool slightly before placing into your fridge. Use whenever you are ready.

Recipe 9:   Chipotle Style Plum Sauce

This is a great preserving dish to make whenever plums come into season. It makes for a great companion to any pork or chicken dish that you make. Either way I know you are going to love it.

Yield: 128 Servings

Cooking Time: 4 Hours and 40 Minutes

List of Ingredients:

- 5 Quarts of Plums, Ripe and Pitted
- 4 Cloves of Garlic, Pressed
- 1 Onion, Finely Diced
- 6 Cups of Sugar, White
- ½ Cup of Vinegar, Apple Cider Variety
- 2 Tablespoons of Chipotle Seasoning, Southwest Variety
- 1 tablespoon of Garlic Seasoning, Roasted Variety
- 1 Jalapeno Pepper, Finely Diced
- 7 teaspoons of Salt, For Taste
- 1 teaspoon of Smoke Flavoring, Liquid Variety
- 8 Canning Jars, With Lids and Rings

AAAAAAAAAAAAAAAAAAAAAAAAAAAAAAAAAAAAAAAAAAAAAAAAAAAAAAAA

Instructions:

1. First place your plums into a colander set inside of a large sized bowl and squeeze to force the juices out. Repeat until all of your plums have been juiced.

2. Pour this juice along with your garlic and onion into a medium sized saucepan and place over medium heat. Bring this mixture to a boil before reducing the heat to low. Continue to simmer until your onions turns translucent.

3. Then pour this mixture into a large sized pot and add in your remaining ingredients. Stir thoroughly until your salt and sugar fully dissolve. Bring this mixture to a boil over medium heat. Once boiling reduce the heat to low and

cook until your mixture is thick in consistency. This should take about 1 ½ hours.

4. After this time remove from heat and allow to cool completely.

5. Pour your mixture into your canning jars and seal with your lids.

6. Boil your jars in some boiling water for the next 10 minutes. Remove and allow to cool slightly before placing into your fridge. Use whenever you are ready.

Recipe 10: Rummage Style Relish

This relish recipe is a dish made with a variety of different vegetables along with some red and green tomatoes to make a relish dish you won't soon forget. For the tastiest results I highly recommend serving this dish the next time you make sandwiches.

Yield: 8 Servings

Cooking Time: 13 Hours and 25 Minutes

List of Ingredients:

- 8 Cups of Green Tomatoes, Cored and Finely Chopped
- 4 Cups of Red Tomatoes, Peeled, Cored and Finely Chopped
- 4 Cups of Cabbage, Roughly Chopped
- 3 Cups of Onion, Finely Sliced
- 2 Cups of Cucumber, Fresh and Finely Chopped
- 1 Cup of Bell Pepper, Green in Color and Finely Chopped
- 1 Cup of Bell Pepper, Red in Color and Finely Chopped
- ½ Cup of Salt, For Taste
- 4 Cups of Brown Sugar, Light and Packed
- 1 tablespoon of Celery Seed
- 1 tablespoon of Cinnamon, Ground Variety
- 1 tablespoon of Mustard Seed
- 1 teaspoon of Ginger, Ground Variety
- 2 Cloves of Garlic, Minced
- ½ teaspoons of Cloves, Ground Variety
- 2 Quarts of Vinegar

AAAAAAAAAAAAAAAAAAAAAAAAAAAAAAAAAAAAAAAAAAAAAAAAAAAAAAAAAAA

Instructions:

1. First use a large sized bowl and mix together your first 7 ingredients until thoroughly combined. Season with your salt and allow to sit for the next 12 to 14 hours. After this time drain and rinse under some running water.

2. Then use a large sized pot and mix together your remaining ingredients until thoroughly combined.

3. Set over medium heat and bring your mixture to a boil, stirring thoroughly to dissolve your sugar.

4. Allow to simmer for the next 10 minutes before adding in your vegetable.

5. Continue to simmer for the next 30 minutes. Remove from heat and allow to cool completely.

6. Pour your mixture into your canning jars and seal with your lids.

7. Boil your jars in some boiling water for the next 10 minutes. Remove and allow to cool slightly before placing into your fridge. Use whenever you are ready.

Recipe 11: Spicy Style Tomato Jam

This dish, while labeled as a jam is more of a relish, but I know you are going to love it. It is filled with a ton of spice and I know it will help satisfy your next spicy craving.

Yield: 32 Servings

Cooking Time: 1 Hour and 40 Minutes

List of Ingredients:

- 3 Pounds of Tomatoes, Fresh
- 1 Gallon of Water, Boiling
- 1 Cup of Vinegar, Cider Variety
- ½ Cup of Apple Juice, Fresh
- 1 ½ Cups of Brown Sugar, Light and Packed
- 1 ½ teaspoons of Salt, For Taste
- ½ teaspoons of Black Pepper, Ground Variety
- ½ teaspoons of Mustard, Ground Variety
- ½ teaspoons of Allspice, Ground Variety
- ½ teaspoons of Cumin, Ground
- ¼ teaspoons of Cayenne Pepper
- 1 Lemon, Cut into Quarters and Sliced Thinly

AAAAAAAAAAAAAAAAAAAAAAAAAAAAAAAAAAAAAAAAAAAAAAAAAAAAA

Instructions:

1. The first thing that you will want to do is place your tomatoes into a large sized pot. Pour in your boiling water and allow to sit for the next 5 minutes. After this time remove your tomatoes and place into a cold water bath until completely cool.

2. Then chop up your tomatoes in a food processor, making sure to reserve any juices.

3. Next add in your remaining ingredients except for your lemon and tomatoes into a large sized saucepan and place over medium heat. Cook until your sugar fully dissolves.

4. Add in your chopped tomatoes and bring this mixture to a boil. Once boiling reduce the heat to low and allow to simmer for the next 30 to 45 minutes or until the liquid has been reduced by at least half.

5. After this time add in your lemon slices and continue to cook for the next 15 minutes.

6. After this time remove from heat and set aside to cool completely.

7. Pour your mixture into your canning jars and seal with your lids.

8. Boil your jars in some boiling water for the next 10 minutes. Remove and allow to cool slightly before placing into your fridge. Use whenever you are ready.

Recipe 12:   Simple Cranberry Butter

This is a festive butter recipe to make and enjoy during the holiday season. This makes for a perfect dish to make to give to your friends and family if you want to give them a meaningful gift.

Yield: 8 Servings

Cooking Time: 15 Minutes

List of Ingredients:

- 2 Tablespoons of Cranberries, Dried
- ½ Cup of Water, Boiling
- ½ Cup of Butter, Soft to The Touch
- 3 Tablespoons of Sugar, Confectioner's Variety

AAAAAAAAAAAAAAAAAAAAAAAAAAAAAAAAAAAAAAAAAAAAAAAAAAAA

Instructions:

1. The first thing that you want to do is stir your boiling water and cranberries together in a large sized bowl. Allow to steep for the next 5 minutes.

2. After this time drain your cranberries and chop them finely.

3. Then use an electric mixer and beat your butter in a separate medium sized bowl until light and fluffy in texture.

4. Add in your sugar and cranberries and beat until thoroughly combined.

5. Pour your mixture into your canning jars and seal with your lids.

6. Boil your jars in some boiling water for the next 10 minutes. Remove and allow to cool slightly before placing into your fridge. Use whenever you are ready.

Recipe 13:   Classic Banana Jam

This is a warm and tropical jam recipe that I know you are going to want to serve with nearly everything that you make. It is perfect when serve with some pancakes or waffles.

Yield: 12 Servings

Cooking Time: 15 Minutes

List of Ingredients:

- 4 Cups of Bananas, Ripe
- 1/3 Cup of Lemon Juice, Fresh
- 2 Tablespoons of Brown Sugar, Light and Packed
- ¼ teaspoons of Nutmeg, Ground

AAAAAAAAAAAAAAAAAAAAAAAAAAAAAAAAAAAAAAAAAAAAAAAAAAA

Instructions:

1. Add all of your ingredients into a blender and blend on the highest setting until smooth in consistency.

2. Place into your canning jars and seal with your lids.

3. Boil your jars in some boiling water for the next 10 minutes. Remove and allow to cool slightly before placing into your fridge. Use whenever you are ready.

Recipe 14:   Acorn Squash Style Butter

If you are a huge fan of different flavors of butter, then this is one dish that I know you are going to love. Once you make this dish keep in mind that it can last up to 2 months in your fridge or up to 6 months in your freezer so plan accordingly.

Yield: 48 Servings

Cooking Time: 3 Hours

List of Ingredients:

- 3 Acorn Squash, cut into Halves and Seeded
- 1 teaspoon of Cinnamon, Ground
- 1 teaspoon of Nutmeg, Ground
- 1 teaspoon of Ginger, Ground
- ½ teaspoons of Cloves, Ground
- 2 ¼ Cups of Brown Sugar, Light and Packed
- 1, 12 Ounce Can of Apple Juice, Concentrated, Frozen and Thawed

AAAAAAAAAAAAAAAAAAAAAAAAAAAAAAAAAAAAAAAAAAAAAAAAAA

Instructions:

1. The first thing that you want to do is preheat your oven to 400 degrees.

2. Next fill up 2 medium sized baking dishes with at least 1 inch of water. Then place your sliced acorn squash into your baking pan and place into your oven to bake until tender to the touch. This should take at least 1 hour. After this time remove and discard your water. Set aside to cool completely.

3. Scoop the flesh out from your squash and add into a blender. Blend on the highest setting until smooth in consistency.

4. Add in your next 4 ingredients and blend again to combine and until thick in consistency.

5. Spoon into a large sized saucepan. Add in your brown sugar and apple juice and continue to cook over medium heat for the next 40 to 45 minutes or until thick in consistency.

6. Remove from heat and allow to cool completely.

7. Pour your mixture into your canning jars and seal with your lids.

8. Boil your jars in some boiling water for the next 10 minutes. Remove and allow to cool slightly before placing into your fridge. Use whenever you are ready.

Recipe 15:   Preserved Carrots and Jalapenos

While I know this dish may seem far from appetizing at first, once you get a taste of it yourself I know you are going to want to make it over and over again. This is the perfect preserving recipe to make to serve alongside your next Mexican inspired dish.

Yield: 12 Servings

Cooking Time: 1 Hour and 20 Minutes

List of Ingredients:

- 1 ½ Cups of Vinegar, White in Color and Distilled
- ¼ Cup of Sugar, White
- 10 Jalapeno Peppers, Sliced Thinly
- 2 Cups of Carrots, Thinly Sliced
- ½ of a Red Onion, Sliced into Thin Rings

AAAAAAAAAAAAAAAAAAAAAAAAAAAAAAAAAAAAAAAAAAAAAAAAAAA

Instructions:

1. The first thing that you will want to do is bring both your sugar and vinegar together in a large sized saucepan. Bring this mixture to a boil over high heat. While cooking make sure to stir thoroughly until your sugar fully dissolves.

2. Then add in your remaining ingredients. Stir to combine.

3. Remove from heat and allow to stand for at least 1 hour.

4. Pour your mixture into your canning jars and seal with your lids.

5. Boil your jars in some boiling water for the next 10 minutes. Remove and allow to cool slightly before placing into your fridge. Use whenever you are ready.

Recipe 16:   Healthy Chia Seed Jam

If you are looking for a healthy jam recipe to enjoy, then this is the perfect jam recipe for you to make. Once you make this dish for yourself you can easily enjoy it right away or store it for later use.

Yield: 10 Servings

Cooking Time: 35 Minutes

List of Ingredients:

- ¼ Cup of Chia Seeds
- ½ Cup of Water, Cold
- 2 Cups of Raspberries, Frozen
- ½ Cup of Blackberries, Frozen
- ½ Cup of Blueberries, Frozen
- 2 Strawberries, Frozen
- 1/3 Cup of Honey, Raw

AAAAAAAAAAAAAAAAAAAAAAAAAAAAAAAAAAAAAAAAAAAAAAAAAAAA

Instructions:

1. The first thing that you will want to do is soak your chia seeds in some water until it resembles a jelly like consistency. This should take about 5 minutes.

2. Then add in your berries and honey into a medium sized saucepan. Place over medium heat and cook until your berries are tender to the touch. This should take about 15 minutes.

3. After this time crush your berries thoroughly until smooth in consistency.

4. Next stir your chia seed mixture into your berry mixture until thoroughly combined.

5. Remove from heat and allow to cool completely.

6. Pour your mixture into your canning jars and seal with your lids.

7. Boil your jars in some boiling water for the next 10 minutes. Remove and allow to cool slightly before placing into your fridge. Use whenever you are ready.

Recipe 17:   Budget Friendly Berry Jam

Just as the name implies this is the perfect jam recipe to make if you find yourself on a very tight budget. For the tastiest results I highly recommend using your favorite flavor of fruit gelatin to make it truly your own recipe.

Yield: 32 Servings

Cooking Time: 25 Minutes

List of Ingredients:

- 4 Cups of Tomato Pulp, Green in Color
- 4 Cups of Sugar, White
- 2, 3 Ounce Packs of Jell-O, Your Favorite Kind

AAAAAAAAAAAAAAAAAAAAAAAAAAAAAAAAAAAAAAAAAAAAAAAAAAAA

Instructions:

1. First use a large sized saucepan placed over medium to high heat. Add in your tomato pulp and sugar and bring this mixture to a boil.

2. Once your mixture is boiling reduce the heat to low and cook for the next 20 minutes, making sure that you stir the mixture once in a while.

3. Remove your mixture from heat and add in your Jell-O, making sure to stir thoroughly to combine and until it completely dissolves. Allow your mixture to cool completely.

4. Pour your mixture into your canning jars and seal with your lids.

5. Boil your jars in some boiling water for the next 10 minutes. Remove and allow to cool slightly before placing into your fridge. Use whenever you are ready.

Recipe 18:   Ginger Flavored Marmalade

While traditional ginger marmalade can sometimes be disappointing due to the texture and aftertaste often left from it, this is not one of those marmalade dishes. Once you get a taste of this marmalade I know you won't be disappointed.

Yield: 30 Servings

Cooking Time: 8 Hours and 35 Minutes

List of Ingredients:

- 3 ½ Cups of Ginger, Fresh and Peeled
- 4 Cups of Water, Cold
- 5 Cups of Sugar, White
- 1, 3 Ounce Package of Pectin, Liquid Variety
- 5, ½ Pint Canning Jars, With Lids and Jars

AAAAAAAAAAAAAAAAAAAAAAAAAAAAAAAAAAAAAAAAAAAAAAAAAAAAA

Instructions:

1. First place your ginger and water into a large sized saucepan. Set over medium heat and bring this mixture to a boil.

2. Once your mixture is boiling reduce the heat to low. Cover and allow to simmer for the next hour and 15 minutes or until your ginger is tender to the touch.

3. Once tender strain your ginger through a fine mesh strainer and drain.

4. Place your ginger into a large sized bowl with your ginger liquid and allow to cool.

5. Place back into your large sized saucepan and add in your sugar. Boil for the next minute, making sure you stir constantly.

6. Add in your liquid pectin and reduce the heat to low. Continue to cook for the next 7 minutes and skim off any excess foam that may form on the top. Remove from heat and allow to cool completely.

7. Pour your mixture into your canning jars and seal with your lids.

8. Boil your jars in some boiling water for the next 10 minutes. Remove and allow to cool slightly before placing into your fridge. Use whenever you are

ready.

Recipe 19: Fresh Tasting Papaya Jam

This is a great tasting preserving recipe to make if you are a huge fan of papaya. Not only is it incredibly delicious, but it is especially excellent when used on toast or waffles.

Yield: 64 Servings

Cooking Time: 5 Hours and 5 Minutes

List of Ingredients:

- 5 Cups of Papaya, Ripe and Mashed
- ¼ Cup of Orange Juice, Fresh
- 1 1/3 of a 1.75 Ounce Package of Pectin, Dry
- 5 Cups of Sugar, White

AAAAAAAAAAAAAAAAAAAAAAAAAAAAAAAAAAAAAAAAAAAAAAAAAAAA

Instructions:

1. First stir together your first 3 ingredients in a large sized pot placed over medium to high heat.

2. Once your mixture begins to boil, add in your sugar and stir constantly as it cooks.

3. Boil for at least 2 to 3 minutes before removing from heat and allowing to cool completely.

4. Pour your mixture into your canning jars and seal with your lids.

5. Boil your jars in some boiling water for the next 10 minutes. Remove and allow to cool slightly before placing into your fridge. Use whenever you are ready.

Recipe 20:   Simple Gooseberry Jam

This preserving jam recipe was passed down to me through my family and has been made through the generations. Made with fresh gooseberries, this is a dish you can make when you are looking to enjoy a different jam you have never tried before.

Yield: 80 Servings

Cooking Time: 30 Minutes

List of Ingredients:

- 2 Quarts of Gooseberries, Fresh
- 6 Cups of Sugar, White
- ½ of a 6 Ounce Container of Pectin, Liquid Variety

AAAAAAAAAAAAAAAAAAAAAAAAAAAAAAAAAAAAAAAAAAAAAAAAAAAAAAA

Instructions:

1. First remove the blossom and stems from your gooseberries. Then puree your gooseberries until smooth in consistency.

2. Place into a large sized pot and add in your sugar.

3. Bring this mixture to a boil over high heat and allow to boil for at least one minute, making sure to stir constantly as it boils.

4. After this time remove from heat and add in your pectin. Stir to combine. Make sure to skim off any foam from your mixture. Allow to cool completely.

5. Pour your mixture into your canning jars and seal with your lids.

6. Boil your jars in some boiling water for the next 10 minutes. Remove and allow to cool slightly before placing into your fridge. Use whenever you are ready.

Recipe 21:   Harvest Time Tomato Marinara Sauce

If you are a huge fan of classic Italian cuisine, then this is the perfect recipe for you. It is incredibly easy to make and makes the most authentic tomato marinara sauce you will ever taste.

Yield: 40 Servings

Cooking Time: 5 Hours

List of Ingredients:

- 25 Pounds of Tomatoes, Plum Variety, Cored and Cut in Halves
- 3 Bay Leaves, Fresh
- 1 ½ Tablespoons of Honey, Raw
- 1 tablespoon of Oregano, Dried
- 1 tablespoon of Salt, For Taste
- 2 teaspoons of Black Pepper, Ground
- ½ Cup of Olive Oil, Extra Virgin Variety
- 1 Pound of Onions, Yellow in Color and Finely Chopped
- 10 Cloves of Garlic, Minced
- 10, 1 Quart Canning Jars, With Lids and Rings
- 10 teaspoons of Salt, For Taste and Evenly Divided
- 1 ¾ Cups of Lemon Juice, Fresh and Evenly Divided

AAAAAAAAAAAAAAAAAAAAAAAAAAAAAAAAAAAAAAAAAAAAAAAAAAAAA

Instructions:

1. First place your first 6 ingredients into a large sized saucepan. Cover with some water and stir thoroughly to combine.

2. Cover and bring this mixture to a boil over medium to high heat.

3. Once boiling reduce the heat to low and allow to simmer for the next 20 minutes uncovered, making sure to stir thoroughly. After this time remove your bay leaves and season to your taste.

4. Next heat up your olive oil in a large sized skillet placed over medium to high heat. Once your oil is hot enough add in your onions and garlic and cook until your onions are soft to the touch. This should take about 10 minutes.

5. Next puree your tomatoes until smooth in consistency and add back to your saucepan. Add in your cooked garlic and onions and cook while uncovered over medium to high heat until your sauce becomes thick in consistency. This should take about 1 to 1 ½ hours.

6. Remove from heat and allow to cool completely.

7. Pour your mixture into your canning jars and seal with your lids.

8. Boil your jars in some boiling water for the next 10 minutes. Remove and allow to cool slightly before placing into your fridge. Use whenever you are ready.

Recipe 22: Carolina Style BBQ Peppers

Once your friends and family get a taste of these BBQ Peppers, I guarantee they will be begging you for the recipe. If you do not want this dish to be too spicy, make sure that you remove the seeds from the pepper.

Yield: 80 Servings

Cooking Time: 20 Minutes

List of Ingredients:

- 2 Cups of Oil, Corn Variety
- 2 Cups of Vinegar, Cider Variety
- 2 Cups of Sugar, White
- 4 Cups of Ketchup, Your Favorite Kind
- 1 Pound of Jalapeno Peppers, Fresh and Sliced into Thin Rings
- Dash of Oregano, Dried
- 1 Clove of Garlic, Minced

AAAAAAAAAAAAAAAAAAAAAAAAAAAAAAAAAAAAAAAAAAAAAAAAAAAA

Instructions:

1. First use a large sized pot and add in your first 4 ingredients and stir thoroughly until your sugar is fully dissolved.

2. Bring this mixture to a boil. Once your mixture is boiling add in your jalapeno peppers. Stir to combine.

3. Reduce your heat to low and allow your mixture to simmer for the next 10 minutes before seasoning with a dash of garlic and oregano. Remove from heat and allow to cool completely.

4. Pour your mixture into your canning jars and seal with your lids.

5. Boil your jars in some boiling water for the next 10 minutes. Remove and allow to cool slightly before placing into your fridge. Use whenever you are ready.

Recipe 23:   Sweet Tasting Kiwi Jam

This delicious kiwi jam recipe incorporates the flavors of mashed kiwi, fresh lemon juice, a touch of sugar and healthy apples to make a jam recipe you won't soon forget!

Yield: 40 Servings

Cooking Time: 12 hours and 40 Minutes

List of Ingredients:

- 24 Kiwis, Peeled and Thoroughly Mashed
- ¾ Cup of Pineapple Juice, Fresh
- ¼ Cup of Lemon Juice, Fresh
- 3 Apples, Unpeeled and Cut into Halves
- 4 Cups of Sugar, White

AAAAAAAAAAAAAAAAAAAAAAAAAAAAAAAAAAAAAAAAAAAAAAAAAAAA

Instructions:

1. First use a large sized saucepan and bring together your first 4 ingredients. Set over medium heat and bring your mixture to a boil.

2. Once your mixture is boiling add in your sugar and stir thoroughly to dissolve.

3. Then reduce the heat to low and continue to simmer for the next 30 minutes.

4. Pour your mixture into your canning jars and seal with your lids.

5. Boil your jars in some boiling water for the next 10 minutes. Remove and allow to cool slightly before placing into your fridge. Use whenever you are ready.

Recipe 24:   Fresh Watermelon Preserves

This is a wonderful preserving recipe that you can enjoy all summer long. This is a great recipe to serve alongside a serving of toast or on some English muffins. Regardless of how you serve it, I know you are going to love it.

Yield: 40 Servings

Cooking Time: 2 Hours and 25 Minutes

List of Ingredients:

- 2 Pounds of Watermelon, Fresh, Seeded and Finely Diced
- 3 Cups of Sugar, White
- 3 Lemons, Fresh, Rinsed, Finely Sliced and Seeded

AAAAAAAAAAAAAAAAAAAAAAAAAAAAAAAAAAAAAAAAAAAAAAAAAAAAAAA

Instructions:

1. Use a large sized stockpot and add in your diced watermelon, sugar and fresh lemons.

2. Bring this mixture to a boil over medium heat. Allow your mixture to boil for the next 2 hours. During this time make sure to stir your mixture occasionally.

3. After this time remove your mixture from heat and set aside to cool completely.

4. Once cooled pour your mixture into your canning jars and seal with your lids.

5. Boil your jars in some boiling water for the next 10 minutes. Remove and allow to cool slightly before placing into your fridge. Use whenever you are ready.

Don't Miss Out!

Scan the QR-Code below and you can sign up to receive emails whenever Molly Mills publishes a new book. There's no charge and no obligation.

Sign Me Up

https://molly.gr8.com